15

DÍA DE LOS MUERTOS

ROSEANNE GREENFIELD THONG

pictures by
CARLES BALLESTEROS

ALBERT WHITMAN & COMPANY
CHICAGO, ILLINOIS

To Francene and Charles—
thanks for celebrating Day of the Dead with me—RGT

To Guillem and all the *ancestros* that take care of him—CB

Library of Congress Cataloging-in-Publication
data is on file with the publisher.

Text copyright © 2015 by Roseanne Greenfield Thong
Pictures copyright © 2015 by Carles Ballesteros
Published in 2015 by Albert Whitman & Company
ISBN 978-0-8075-1566-2
Printed in China
10 9 8 7 6 5 4 3 2 HH 20 19 18 17 16 15

Design by Jordan Kost

For more information about Albert Whitman & Company,
visit our web site at www.albertwhitman.com.

It's *Día de Los Muertos*, the sun's coming round,
as *niños* prepare in each pueblo and town.
For today we will honor our dearly departed
with *celebraciónes*—it's time to get started!

At home we've adorned our *altares* with care.
They're heaped with *recuerdos* and good things
to share…

Sweet *calaveras*, so sugary white—
they give toothy smiles, but never a fright.

A black-and-white photo of Grandpa Padilla,
who's riding on horseback just like Pancho Villa!
And toys for remembering small *angelitos*,
a train and a dollhouse are both *favoritos*.

Then off to the graveyard we head with *ofrendas* and colorful blankets to make *meriendas*.

We carry *incienso* and *velas* to burn
that will guide spirits back for their yearly return.

CEMETERY

And bursts of *caléndulas*, fragrant and bright—
the color of sunsets and gold candlelight.

A path of *pétalos* will help lead our guest
to pillows and blankets for taking a rest.

Above we hang streamers of *papel picado*
that wave in the breeze like a rainbow *pintado*.

BRAULIO

We giggle at paper-cut banners we like—
esqueletos riding a horse cart or bike!

ROSARIO

We share in the foods that our guests loved to eat—
fresh fruit and *tamales*, a holiday treat.

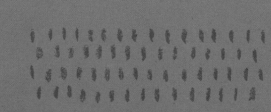

And clay pots of Grandmother's fresh chicken stew,
with mugs of *atole*, a chocolaty brew.

ROSARIO

But everyone's favorite is sugary bread,
called *pan de muerto*, with bones of the dead,

that offers our travelers a much-needed snack
from the weary *viaje* that brought them all back.

Then after our lunch comes the part we love most—
putting on makeup to dress like a ghost!

In veils and costumes we join the parade.
Although we wear *huesos*, no one is afraid.

Gilberto has scars and a special *corona*.
Anabel looks like the real *La Llorona*.

Joaquin's snow-white *barba* sweeps down to the floor,
while Luz looks like someone we've all seen before!

And just as the marigold clouds end the day,
dancers and *músicos* come out to play.
They wear special shells that go clickety-clack,
to wake up *espíritus*, calling them back.

As candle flames glisten, our smiles are bright.
Our *ancestros* know we are with them tonight.

They return to their world without sadness or fear,
knowing they'll stay in our hearts till next year.

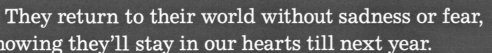

About Día de los Muertos

Day of the Dead, or *Día de los Muertos* is celebrated on November 1 or 2 in Mexico and other Latin American countries and communities. It is a day to remember and honor the dead and welcome their spirits home for a night. The emphasis of this day is on the joy of life rather than the sadness of death. Some families build home altars, while others visit cemeteries to hold picnics and spend time with departed souls.

Home altars are adorned with photos, flowers, candles, or the deceased's favorite possessions and foods. Families also set out sweet egg bread known as *pan de muerto* or bread of the dead. It is formed into various shapes from skulls to rabbits or covered with frosted white sugar to look like skeleton bones. Sugar skulls, or *calaveras*, are given as gifts and placed on altars. The skulls, often sold in open-air markets, are colorfully decorated with icing, bright foil, frosting, and the names of loved ones.

Families head to cemeteries to clean and decorate gravesites. Graves can be adorned with candles, offerings, flowers, and incense. In some villages, paths of bright marigold petals lead from the cemetery to individual homes. The petals' strong scent is said to guide spirits home. Colorful paper-cut banners known as *papel picado* depict comical scenes like skeletons on horseback or ghosts riding bicycles.

Offerings of favorite foods and possessions are displayed in hopes of enticing spirits back for a visit. Stuffed animals, toy cars, cookies, or sodas might be left for young *angelitos*. Chicken mole, tequila, or *atole*, a hot chocolate beverage, might be set out for older souls.

Day of the Dead traditions are said to be over 3,000 years old, stemming from ancient traditions of the Aztecs and other pre-Columbian groups. These ancient peoples believed in the afterlife and viewed death as part of life—something to be accepted and embraced. When the Spanish arrived in the Americas, they changed the celebration date from the summer to fall so it would coincide with All Saints' and All Souls' Day (November 1 and 2). In this way, the Aztec and Catholic cultures became intermingled.

To this day, children and adults celebrate Día de los Muertos by having fun—painting faces, dressing up like ghosts, and mocking death. In this way, the whole *pueblo*, or community, can joyfully connect with departed relatives and friends.

Glossary

altares - altars built for honoring and remembering the dead

ancestros - ancestors

angelitos - departed children, or "little angels"

atole - a hot, masa-based (cornmeal) beverage sweetened with chocolate

barba - beard

calaveras - decorative sugar skulls given as offerings and gifts

caléndulas - marigold flowers

celebraciónes - celebrations

corona - crown

espíritus - spirits

esqueletos - skeletons

favoritos - favorites

huesos - bones

incienso - incense

La Llorona - legend of a woman who wanders the earth for eternity, crying as she searches for her family

meriendas - light afternoon meals; picnics

músicos - musicians

niños - children

ofrendas - offerings

Pancho Villa - legendary bandit and folk hero during the Mexican Revolution

pan de muerto - bread of the dead

papel picado - cut-paper banners

pétalos - flower petals

pintado - painted

pueblo - community, village, nation

recuerdos - memories

velas - candles

viaje - journey